What Others Are Saying about Child of God:

Raven tells her story with passion: a wonderful balance of personal testimony and rays of hope. The questions of self-reflection are powerful and a unique way of challenging the reader to not just read Raven's story but apply her wisdom and revelation to their own life. By the end of this book, you will not only know this powerful woman of God better, but you will gain a more intimate relationship with our Lord and Savior, Jesus Christ.

— Erica Fite

Beloved Friend and Children's Pastor

"Therefore, if anyone is in Christ, the new creation has come: the old has gone, the new is here!" (2 Cor. 5:17) Raven's story shines of this truth. We all go through many phases in our journey with God. I love how she expresses it through this book. I hope you enjoy her story as much as I did.

— Darren Smith

Beloved Bible Student and Teacher

Child of GOD

Walking In Victory by Walking
in Your Identity in Christ

Raven Kask

Author photo credits to Stephanie Velasquez.

Published in the United States of America.

ISBNs: 979-8-9986342-0-8 (Paperback)

979-8-9986342-2-2 (Ebook)

This book is dedicated to everyone who's been lost in their identity, tried to fit a mold, or lost their sense of self, just know that God made you a masterpiece and he has a plan for your life.

Also, to all of those who loved me back to life, beginning in 2018 when I was at my lowest, my family, my church, the recovery community, and all of those I now call friends, thank you!

Contents

Introduction

I f you have ever questioned who you are or wondered if God accepts you, or if what you are going through has caused you to question your salvation, this book is for you! I have gone around this same mountain—more than once. I want to share with you what the Lord has taught me and how He helped me break the cycle in order to move forward in my life and into the plans He has for me.

I answered yes many times to those questions; and, truthfully, I have given myself to Jesus time and time again. I have learned—and am still learning—that there is a difference between getting saved and the process of sanctification through Jesus Christ by the power of the Holy Spirit. Each time I failed, I found myself trapped in the cycle of condemnation, doubt, and fear, rather than receiving conviction and the hope and direction the Holy Spirit had for me. It is a trust thing.

In this book, I share a portion of my journey with you—how I came to Christ—and paint a picture of what it looks like to live trapped in a false identity (based on personal experience) versus what it looks like to walk in your God-given identity. I also want to share some personal insights from the Word of God surrounding our identity in Christ. My prayer is that, through this revelation, shame, guilt, and accusation from both the devil and yourself will stop! I pray that you will allow the Holy Spirit to influence your heart and tell you who you really are. I pray that you will learn how to walk a surrendered, obedient life in victory with Christ and that you will know what it truly means to be a child of God.

Chapter 1: A New Name

What is the new name that God is giving you?" This was a challenging question that my home Bible study leader asked me. We were having our weekly Wednesday meeting, and the topic was repentance. I had asked a question, and I'm not sure if he heard the uncertainty in my voice, but the Holy Spirit knew.

My identity in Christ was the thing that held me when I didn't know what was what. Thinking about the hardest time in my Christian walk, I remember that things felt very shaky, and I began to lose myself. During the trying times, though I did not know it then, what brought me through was my identity in Christ. I knew that I could turn to Him and pursue Him. When nothing else felt right, Jesus did. And Jesus *is* my identity. I am now dead to myself and alive in Christ.

Christ is my anchor. The things I do, and the people I am with, do not define me; Christ does. It is critical that we know who we are in Christ; otherwise, we will continue to search and take on wrong identities through people, places, and things. This is ever-changing as we begin to take on identities that we were not meant to assume. When our identity comes from other things and other people, we are on very shaky ground.

People and circumstances are always changing. Imagine doing something that you feel it is time to let go of, but because it has become your identity, you cannot, and then you find yourself completely drained.

It is okay to do things, hang out with people, etc., but if I am receiving my identity from them, what happens when they are no longer a part of my life and God tells me to move? I will lose a part of me. I may even become disobedient because that was where I found my identity. Now imagine if I make Christ my identity. When things change—and they will—that is okay. When He tells me to move, I can move.

Those things are not who I am; they are only things I did or sometimes do. I am not Raven, the one who does this or that and hangs out with so and so, but also goes to church and reads her Bible. I am a woman of God—a child of God who has done things, been in relationships, and participated in various endeavors.

I found that not knowing my identity when I was young was detrimental. Because I did not know who I was, I took on other personas. I remember always wanting to *find myself* and have a cool identity and cool quirks.

I wanted to be different but cool. I found my identity in the things I had, the practices I did, and even the people around me. If I ran track and field, that became an identity I took on. If I made crafts to sell at school—my best friend and I sewed little stuffies and made bracelets—that became a part of my identity. When I was dating a guy, being his girlfriend became my identity. The clothes I wore, the family I grew up in, etc., consumed me because I gave myself away to all of those things. I remember being very upset when I had to wear a pair of pink sweats that my mom got me when I was in kindergarten.

I found my identity in the things I had, the practices I did, and even the people around me.

Looking back now, I think it was because I found my identity in the clothes I wore. I was beyond upset and remember arriving at school with puffed-up, red eyes like it was the end of the world. I always wanted to be that person who was always in a sport or always whatever. I wanted those things so when people thought of me, they thought of those things that represented me. I thought that somehow that made me cool. For me, nothing ever felt like I wanted to do it forever; I just wasn't that girl, and I hated that. So, searching I continued.

I knew about God, but I did not understand that He could be my identity. I just thought of Him like Santa Claus: kind of incognito and comes out at certain times. For me, it was bedtime prayers and Sundays. And then, He only cared if you are naughty or nice, but mostly naughty. You get rewarded with heaven if you are good and rewarded hell if you are bad. I know that is bad theology, but in my simple kid mind, that was it.

I knew that God was real, and I never doubted that. I am so glad that my parents introduced me to Him. In this world that likes to say that God is not real, or has a hard time believing in a God they cannot see, I have always known! However, I did not know Jesus personally, therefore, I had no access to the power of the Holy Spirit who changes us and works on our behalf. I knew that Jesus died on the cross to forgive my sins, but I did not know what that meant for my own life or how to apply it. I did not even know that I could.

So when life happened, I did not have a true lifeline. Ever since I can remember, in kindergarten at least, I did not know my identity in Christ. I knew we went to church, but that was it. It was not everything. And I think it is a process that as we get to know him better and deeper, He becomes our identity more and more. I believe even knowing that is something many Christians could be missing.

So, going through life, something that I began partaking of was *trouble!* I was doing things I was not supposed to do. That was becoming my identity, and to me, it kind of fit. I was becoming good at doing things I was not supposed to do because I did not understand the sinful nature. We are inherently bad at birth because of Adam and Eve messing up in the garden. Paul tells us that we have a sinful nature inside of us, and it is only through Jesus Christ that we can overcome it.

> For I know that good itself does not dwell in me, that is, in my sinful nature. For I have the desire to do what is good, but I cannot carry it out. What a wretched man I am! Who will rescue me from this body that is subject to death? Thanks be to God, who delivers me through Jesus Christ our Lord! (Romans 7:18, 24-25 NIV)

I was not born good and then turned bad. I was born bad and am someone who, through Jesus, has been made good. I had this backward. I liked to think of myself in some ways as a good kid; I was generous, and on the outside, I tried to be good. I did well in school, excelling usually, but on the inside, I was not the same person. My dad had given me a promise ring in kindergarten. When I received that, I also received shame because I already had crushes on boys. I did not feel worthy to take the ring. Right there was an open door to a false identity, which was a dirty, boy-crazy, secret-holder, and rejected by my dad and God. That unhealthy identity trait was one of the main ones I internalized, and it followed me for a very long time.

During the Bible study mentioned at the beginning of this chapter, God prompted my leader to ask me that question: "What is the new name that God is giving you?" I did not have an immediate answer and went home thinking about it. Nothing came to mind until 4:00 a.m. I woke up, and I was drawn out of my bed and to the couch. Then He told me who I am: a child of God.

Chapter 2: A New Identity

What are some lies that you have internalized from as early on as you can remember? Do they still follow you? Are they still affecting your life in negative ways today?

I pretty much always had a boyfriend or a crush. My poor brothers! I would always tell them who I liked. Even with friends, I constantly talked about boys. That was pretty much the hot topic. My friends, I could tell, were becoming annoyed, so I began to feel like an outsider. I began to feel like other people could not understand me; they just didn't get me. At least internally, that is what I was believing without realizing it. And it kept progressing.

As the lies grew and more were added, I was turning more into the type of person I was not meant to be. As I got older, those parts of me intensified. What began with hiding my journals because I wrote who I had a crush on eventually led to sneak texting. I was then sneaking out, running away, and skipping school to be with boys.

When something becomes our identity, it grows—especially if it is sinful nature. It is like a cancer, and what we feed grows.

Is there anything you are feeding that needs to die? What could become a problem if you keep feeding it?

So as the wrong identity emerged, I was growing up with the wrong people, places, and things too. I remember distinctly though, having those moments where I kept doing things I did not want to be doing. Like Paul says:

> For I do not do the good I want to do, but
> the evil I do not want to do—this I keep
> on doing. (Romans 7:19 NIV)

At that point in my life, I was a slave to sin, not Christ, like I should have been. I did not have the power to overcome because I did not have Jesus, therefore I did not receive the Holy Spirit. I was not yet an overcomer like I am today. Today I can take the stance as an overcomer because I now have the Spirit of God living inside of me. I have allowed Him in, and He has permission to change me from the inside out.

Even when we are walking through the sanctification process and it feels heavy, and I fail, my identity is in Christ. I have to remember that I am righteous because of Jesus. Those struggles are not my identity. That is why God is bringing me through the process of shaving them off. I did not have this gift then; I kind of accepted my lot, you could say, and went for it, though I still knew deep down it was not the real me. These lies and the lack of identity led me to eventually be full of rejection, shame, and fear. I became addicted to drugs and isolated from anyone who truly cared for me or could help me. I had two kids that I could not care for, and I was in a relationship that was hurting me. I had hit rock bottom.

I had gotten to a place where I hated what I was doing. I was so ashamed I hung out with those who were doing the things I hated that I avoided seeing anyone who could have been good for me. I wondered how I could do what I was doing, but because it had become such a part of my identity, it was hard to separate myself. I was not doing the things I needed to be doing, like being a mother. My false identity led me to chase other things like trying to hold things together with my boyfriend, focusing on how I could get high next, and how I could better hide myself.

I have identified five dangers of false identities: trouble letting go, anxiety, turning to false comforts and idols, being performance-driven, and isolation. Any one of these can be dangerous, but every one of them can be overcome.

Trouble Letting Go

This can manifest in many different ways, ranging from big to little. Some of the ways that it came out for me, in particular, was letting go of relationships that were not right because they either violated God's Word, brought compromise, or caused me to settle. You can say I was that girl who stayed with a guy no matter what, as long as he *loved me*. Everything about it was wrong, but I stayed by their side. Because of this, I had trouble letting go, and I stayed in a wrong relationship for nine years.

Some of the false identities I had were *broken*, *not worthy*, *drug dependent*, and *boy crazy*. I stayed for all of the wrong reasons. I had been involved in something that I felt the prompting of God to leave, but I couldn't. Why not? Because it had become such a huge part of my identity that when God said to move, I could not move.

Anxiety

Another horrible side effect of having a false identity is anxiety. Oh boy, anxiety comes when we are not trusting God! It is an indication for us that something is off. Having a false identity throws this all out of whack because we were never meant to be doing what we are doing. When I was doing what I knew deep down I shouldn't, I was anxiety-ridden. It is not only things we think we should not be doing, but also not being able to adjust things because we have misplaced our identity. We need to have our identity in God so we can listen and not ignore the indicators He gives us. If we are doing something that results in anxiety, but we ignore it because we have our identity placed in that thing, we are off track, and we feel that. God made us to be in tune with Him and to walk with Him.

False Comforts and Idols

It is easy to get off track when other things are leading us; we often turn to false comforts and idols as well. In fact, a false identity can become an idol. It is a cycle: we believe lies, do bad things, feel shame, receive the wrong identity, look for comfort in the wrong places, are not satisfied, and then start the cycle over again. If we are not interrupted by Jesus, the cycle could go around and around. It has to stop somewhere—ideally with identifying the lies. If we can believe and walk in the truth of who we are, we will be saved from a lot of hurt. We have to know the true Comforter though. Other things cannot satisfy us. It is like when Jesus was talking with the Samaritan woman at the well. She was drawing water, and Jesus began to reveal Himself to her.

> Jesus replied, "Anyone who drinks this water will soon become thirsty again. But those who drink the water I give will never be thirsty again. It becomes a fresh, bubbling spring within them, giving them eternal life." (John 4:13-14)

She wanted this water, and once Jesus revealed Himself to her and she believed, she went and told everyone in town. I have heard people say that the first evangelist was a woman. Well, here I am to say that Jesus truly satisfies. I remember feelings of restlessness and discontent before knowing Jesus. My idols (false identities) failed me; they left me more thirsty than when I began.

My idols (false identities) failed me; they left me more thirsty than when I began.

Performance

One of the ugliest things we can become is performance driven. We should be compelled by God's love in everything, not driven by performance. I think today this is a difficult one. Coming from where I have been, I can take on that identity that subconsciously believes I need to fix and make up for what I have done. It has caused me to be a bit too hard on myself, and phrases like "I knew better" became weapons I used against myself.

I absolutely believe that we are to strive to be like Christ, but this has to come from knowing that He is our identity. If we are fighting from a place of victory rather than for it, things get easier. It is easy to have these expectations, not meet them, and then get overwhelmed and want to give up. Or you can go the other way and drive yourself into the ground. If we have a healthy balance of who we are in Christ and can fight our battles this way, we can receive the grace God has for us to walk in victory. It can be easy to want to stray when we are not living up to who we think we should be.

Isolation

Isolation keeps us away from our loved ones—ones who could help us and ones that we could help in return. As I mentioned earlier, when I was in the depths of where lies had led me, I isolated myself. I tended to ignore and stay away from my family. There was one instance in particular when my family had not seen me in months, so they just showed up at my work to ask my boss if I was still working there and then left without saying anything to me. They were checking to see if I was alive because I had not been in contact. There was also a period when I did not see my kids for three months. I did not want to see them because I was afraid it would make me want to be clean. Isolation lies to us to keep us bound and in self-pity. It likes to keep us in the dark, so we feel *safe*. I avoided any contact with anyone who was not doing what I was doing.

When I began to need help, I reached out to public organizations, eventually my dad, and there were a couple of people I began to open up about what I was going through. I believe this was the beginning of my freedom. The devil would love nothing more than to keep us isolated and quiet about our struggles, which is very dangerous for us.

A man who isolates himself seeks his own desire; He rages against all wise judgment. (Proverbs 18:1 NKJV)

Once I was able to be around people who could help me, things began to shift. I began to see hope, and I believe this hope gave me the strength to pray that bold prayer that led me to finally personally meet Jesus.

Do you find yourself identifying with any of these five dangers? Which ones and why? How can you begin to walk in your identity in Christ and apply that to these areas instead?

Thankfully, when you meet the real Jesus, you receive a Helper and Friend—the Holy Spirit. The living God comes to live inside of us, and we receive power to overcome every enemy. I finally expressed my true need for God after praying a bold prayer along the lines of: *Show me this isn't for me*. I think the importance was not in the wording of the prayer but the posture of my heart.

I was truly desperate, and God heard my cry. He came in and pulled me out of the pit as I recognized my need for Him. This began the journey of a walk with Christ. The beautiful thing is that because Jesus is the only One who fits inside the God-sized hole in us, He can penetrate the darkness in our lives, satisfy us, and bring true change. He becomes a part of us once we believe and accept Him into our life. Then our journey with true identity can begin.

Chapter 3: A New Family

Now that we have a true identity, we can let go and have peace, healthy relationships, true comfort, and the freedom to make mistakes. Once I allowed Jesus in, I was able to let go of the relationship that had held me in bondage for nine years, the drugs, and the people. This was the first time in my attempts to get sober that I was able to let go of some of the things that kept me in bondage. It was very freeing and made room in my life for the good things that God wanted to bring in. He doesn't just take something away; He wants to replace it with something better! Once I received Jesus and I began to slowly put my trust in Him, He became my Master—not the things that previously held me in bondage.

Before, since I had not personally met Jesus, sin was my master. And since I had not received Him and His grace, this disqualified me because Jesus is the payment for sin. I am not saying to go on sinning, but we now have grace that allows us to recognize sin, agree that it is less than God has for us, ask for help, and allow and receive the changes Jesus wants to make in us. We now live a lifestyle of repentance. When we don't have Jesus, we are condemned already from birth.

> God saved you by his grace when you believed. And you can't take credit for this; it is a gift from God. Salvation is not a reward for the good things we have done, so none of us can boast about it. For we are God's masterpiece. He has created us anew in Christ Jesus, so we can do the good things he planned for us long ago. (Ephesians 2:8-10)

> For you created my inmost being; you knit me together in my mother's womb. I praise you because I am fearfully and wonderfully made; your works are wonderful, I know that full well. (Psalm 139:13-14 NIV)

In Genesis, God makes it known that we are made in His image. Now we can stand knowing that God made us a certain way, and sin taints that!

Knowing who we are while overcoming sin is key! When we can fight from a place of victory with the power of the Holy Spirit, and grace, then we are overcomers.

We must know who we are in Christ! We need to know that we are children, and God is our Abba Father! We have to understand the relationship we have with

Chapter 3: A New Family

Jesus. If when we were still sinners, Christ loved and died for us, how much more now that we are seeking Him and have received Him into our life after we recognize who He is and that He has forgiven us? There was a time in my walk with God when someone suggested digging deeper into the heart of the Father. This was hard for me because, while I have a loving dad, there were trials in our relationship. I am not blaming my parents at all, but the reality is that our relationship with our earthly father does impact our relationship with our heavenly Father.

With all the turmoil I had, and the behavior problems stemming from rejection and a lack of identity, it was a constant battle with my parents doing their best to discipline me. A stronghold formed in my mind that if I was bad, I was not loved or liked, but trapped. What I mean by trapped is that I was often grounded because of all the trouble I was in. If you ask some of my childhood friends, I bet they would tell you that I was grounded a lot! So it was this weird dynamic; if I felt my dad's anger, I did not feel wanted at home because of my actions. I got the cold shoulder, yet I had to be home because I was in trouble. I felt unwanted, yet I had to be there. I eventually carried that into my walk with the Lord. I thought that if I acted right, He would love me, when in reality, His love would set me free.

At that point in my walk, the way I related to God was also like a trapped feeling. It felt like it was suffocating me rather than bringing me life. Again, this was a lie. Jesus came to bring us life and life more abundantly (John 10:10). His love and forgiveness do not restrict me; they protect me. I had this so wrong. Any good father—even my dad—does not want us to sin. But I think it is equally important to know that God is a good Father and to understand why He does not want you to sin. I understood sin to be things God does not want us to do because He was a funsucker or something; but no, He understands heartbreak. He sees the bigger picture, and He sees the lie the Enemy is going to yell out at you the moment you give in. He sees that sin causes trouble and pain in our lives. That helps me so much. When we understand this, we can begin to walk in repentance and victory over sin.

Confession and honesty are important. God already knows everything, but there is forgiveness through confessing to Him. The apostle John states this clearly:

> If we confess our sins to him, he is faithful and just to forgive our sins and to cleanse us from all wickedness. (1 John 1:9)

When we are honest with God, He can begin the work He wants to do in us; but if we are justifying our actions or we are in denial, how can He work? David is so relatable:

> When I refused to confess my sin, my body wasted away, and I groaned all day long. Day and night your hand of dis-

cipline was heavy on me. My strength evaporated like water in the summer heat. Finally, I confessed all my sins to you and stopped trying to hide my guilt. I said to myself, "I will confess my rebellion to the LORD." And you forgave me! All my guilt is gone. (Psalm 32:3-5)

How beautiful is that? God is faithful and wants us to come to Him again and again, and not settle for anything less than His best.

God is faithful and wants us to come to Him again and again, and not settle for anything less than His best.

It is good to acknowledge that we know something is a sin. James says:

So get rid of all the filth and evil in your lives, and humbly accept the word God has planted in your hearts, for it has the power to save your souls. (James 1:21)

The bottom line is that if God's Word says it, then it is the truth, even if it rubs us the wrong way and exposes us. It can feel vulnerable and even scary when you are being called to release something to God. Be led by the Spirit in this because He will give you strength for the thing He is working out of you or asking you to give up. My pastor says that the devil will always tell you what you need to give up but never what you will gain in Christ!

Receiving what God wants to do in your life, putting action to the desires He is giving you, and turning away from your old ways is the path to overcoming sin—this is repentance. We do not do this by willpower! The first time I had this revelation was when I prayed that prayer of admitting my need for help, and God began to change my desires. I began to not want to do what I was doing.

Before God intervened, this looked different. My previous attempts to quit were based more on radical emotions or circumstances. I felt deep down that what I was doing was wrong, but I had not yet had a heart change. I was in a cycle that went something like this: I would buy some drugs, use a little, get relief, feel super regretful, cry, question my life, determine how I was going to quit, make all these resolutions, be proud of myself, throw away the rest, waste money, get a craving, go into panic, begin to regret my decision, and then buy more drugs the next day. It was like that phrase: *white knuckling it*. I was relying on my own will. I was relying on my own strength. I had not yet allowed God into my situation, so I was not in full surrender to Him.

Chapter 3: A New Family

Underneath the symptoms of sin are heart issues and deep places that need to be healed, often from childhood. Generational hurts—or whatever they are—if those wounds are left unhandled and unsurrendered to God, they will cause you to try to cope in negative ways. The work needs to begin on the inside, and then strength will begin to rise. I remember the last day I used meth, and afterward, my cry out to God. I actually did not want to get high, but because of habit and who I was with, I still did, though I distinctly remember not wanting to do it.

Pay attention when you are asking God to help you and He begins exchanging His desires for yours. Are you just now doing things out of habit or because of the crowd you are with? Sometimes when you change direction and leave behind your old life, you will also have to leave behind some of the people you were with. God wants to be your Father, and He wants to give you a new family who will love you and support you on your journey.

As I allowed God in and my ideas were challenged, I began to change. When we are in Christ, we learn and grow in His ways. I believe that because of my repentant and willing heart, I was able to say yes to drug treatment. The acceptance that I needed in order to take some action toward what I wanted was important. I understood that my way of doing and believing had led me to the place I describe in this book. I had to put off the old nature and put on the new nature. The Word of God tells us:

> Let the Holy Spirit guide your lives. Then
> you won't be doing what your sinful na-
> ture craves. (Galatians 5:16)

This means that as we turn *to* what God is leading us to do, we can turn *from* sin and repent. I have been in that place where I wanted what I wanted and that was it. As much as we love God, the sinful nature still wants what it wants. You may be at a point where you need to look into deliverance if it has become too strong, because you cannot give in.

The amazing thing though is that David shows us by example that we can ask God to give us a willing heart.

> Create in me a clean heart, O God. Renew
> a loyal spirit within me. (Psalm 51:10)

It is a bold prayer to ask God to help us to be will-ing. I even questioned if this was okay. I was a bit wor-ried even admitting that I just did not want to do what I believed God was asking me to do, but He confirmed that I could ask for His help at any time. That is the basis of it all and the beauty of Jesus Christ. We cannot do this on our own. As we surrender and submit to God, the Holy Spirit is the One changing us.

> And I am certain that God, who began the
> good work within you, will continue his
> work until it is finally finished on the day
> when Christ Jesus returns. (Philippians 1:6)

Chapter 3: A New Family

There is our part, and there is God's part; we never do anything alone.

Chapter 4: A New Freedom

The more I grow in Christ, the more I realize that He is everything. Isaiah tells us that He will be called Wonderful Counselor, Mighty God, Everlasting Father, and Prince of Peace (Isaiah 9:6). That is just scratching the surface of who He is. No one can come to the Father except through Jesus, which means that if we don't know Jesus, we can't know God. Pastor Vlad Savchuk explains the importance of glorifying Jesus and how that changed his whole walk and ministry with Him. In his book, he describes a time at a retreat where he was expected to speak, but the lights went out, and he began to be flooded with anxiety, unworthiness, and frustration. He explains that he even felt like he had no spiritual power. But when God spoke to him, his view changed:

> You don't need electricity, lights, a microphone, or even heat to have the Holy Spirit show up. All you need is the cross. Jesus must be glorified….I took the focus

off myself and turned my attention to Jesus, reminding myself that all the angels and inhabitants of heaven sing, "Worthy is the Lamb" (Revelation 5:11-12). Everything shifted in my soul and faith rose! A river of living water started to flow out of my spirit.[1]

Jesus, Jesus, Jesus is all I can think of.

A recent revelation, and maybe just through deeper study, I am seeing that Jesus *is* the Word. So when we are in the Word, we are getting to know Jesus. This gives me great hope for myself and for others. The Bible tells us:

> Do not conform to the pattern of this world, but be transformed by the renewing of your mind. (Romans 12:2 NIV)

We renew our mind with Scripture—the sword of the Spirit. When you get into the Word, it is important to ask the Holy Spirit to reveal what He is saying in the passage of Scripture before we read because we do not want to lean on our own understanding. Many times, I found the revelation I needed in the Word of God. We should always be in the Word because it is a guide for our life.

> Your word is a lamp to guide my feet and a light for my path. (Psalm 119:105)

1. Savchuk, Vlad, *Host the Holy Ghost* (Vladimir Savchuk, 2023), 15.

Chapter 4: A New Freedom

A time when God brought revelation by speaking to me directly through His Word—a rhema word—was really on the topic of this whole book: security and identity.

> Only those whose hands and hearts are pure, who do not worship idols and never tell lies. They will receive the LORD's blessing and have a right relationship with God their savior. (Psalm 24:4-5)

At first glance, I thought about how unqualified I felt. I was sure that I was not considered pure in the Lord's eyes. But before I accepted that as truth, I asked the Holy Spirit to lead me in what He was saying. And He led me to this verse:

> I pray that your love will overflow more and more, and that you will keep on growing in knowledge and understanding. For I want you to understand what really matters, so that you may live PURE and BLAMELESS lives until the day of Christ's return. (Philippians 1:9-10, author's emphasis)

That is how I live a blameless life—by growing in Christ. But I would not have gotten to this point of freedom if I was not in His Word and growing in His grace and knowledge. This is something we get by abiding in Him and in His Word.

This brings me to the next key—worship. It is not just music. Worship does many things: it helps us take our eyes off of ourselves, it gets us openly declaring God's truth, and we glorify Jesus and display our trust in Him. Worship gets us into a place of remembrance and gives us hope. I believe it is a powerful faith builder.

I recall a season in my walk when I felt unworthy to worship, but the Holy Spirit began to put these words into my heart: I will not wait to worship. I will not wait to praise You. I will not wait till I feel it. I will not wait for the breakthrough.

These words were profound because they reminded me that I worship Jesus because He is Jesus, not because of myself. There is something powerful about taking our eyes off of ourselves and putting our eyes on Jesus. Walking through the process of sanctification can hurt, but the Word tells us that He will give us a garment of praise for the spirit of heaviness (Isaiah 61:3 NKJV).

There is something powerful about taking our eyes off of ourselves and putting our eyes on Jesus.

Do not fall into the trap of condemnation. I must say that this is hard for me. Because I so radically came to Christ, I want everything to be radical! That is not a bad thing. Jesus is our example of perfection, which we strive for in Christ. But we will make mistakes, fall short, and not meet our expectations, so we have to make room for ourselves to grow.

God showed me something amazing regarding this: Sometimes we can make ourselves, our mistakes, and our downfalls idols. When we begin to think bigger of our failings than of God, it is not right. They have then become giants in our life. What I need to do when I recognize those things in me is look to God, who delivered me from doing meth, and think, *Okay, He's got this too*! I need to recognize who God is and then get back up again. In worship, we find the freedom to do that. It helps us to focus on God and remember His faithfulness. That's why I say that worship is a faith builder.

There was a long period in my walk when I would try so hard, make resolutions, say I will not do this or that, but then I would fail. I let shame, guilt, and condemnation take over. This reminds me of Galatians where Paul just lays it straight. He talks about his conversion: He was one way, but then he became a whole new person with a whole new name! He talks about the law and how it can become like a yolk of slavery.

> Did you receive the Holy Spirit by obeying the law of Moses? Of course not! You received the Spirit because you believed the message you heard about Christ. How foolish can you be? After starting your

new lives in the Spirit, why are you now trying to become perfect by your own human effort? Have you experienced so much for nothing? Surely it was not in vain, was it? (Galatians 3:2-4)

Then in verse ten it goes on to say:

But those who depend on the law to make them right with God are under his curse, for the Scriptures say, "Cursed is everyone who does not observe and obey all the commands that are written in God's Book of the Law." So it is clear that no one can be made right with God by trying to keep the law. For the Scriptures say, "It is through faith that a righteous person has life." This way of faith is very different from the way of law, which says, "It is through obeying the law that a person has life."

But Christ has rescued us from the curse pronounced by the law. When he was hung on the cross, he took upon himself the curse for our wrongdoing. For it is written in the Scriptures, "Cursed is everyone who is hung on a tree." Through Christ Jesus, God has blessed the Gentiles with the same blessing he promised to Abraham, so that we who are believers might receive the promised Holy Spirit through faith. (Galatians 3:10-14)

These scriptures bring life and remind me of John 15:4. Jesus tells us that if we abide in Him, He will also abide in us! And also Colossians:

> And now, just as you accepted Christ Jesus as your Lord, you must continue to follow him. Let your roots grow down into him, and let your lives be built on him. Then your faith will grow strong in the truth you were taught, and you will overflow with thankfulness. Don't let anyone capture you with empty philosophies and high-sounding nonsense that come from human thinking and from the spiritual powers of this world, rather than from Christ. For in Christ lives all the fullness of God in a human body. So you also are complete through your union with Christ, who is the head over every ruler and authority. (Colossians 2:6-10)

And in the next chapter, we read:

> So put to death the sinful, earthly things lurking within you. Have nothing to do with sexual immorality, impurity, lust, and evil desires. Don't be greedy, for a

41

greedy person is an idolater, worshiping the things of this world. Because of these sins, the anger of God is coming. You used to do these things when your life was still part of this world. But now is the time to get rid of anger, rage, malicious behavior, slander, and dirty language. Don't lie to each other, for you have stripped off your old sinful nature and all its wicked deeds. Put on your new nature, and be renewed as you learn to know your Creator and become like him. In this new life, it doesn't matter if you are a Jew or a Gentile, circumcised or uncircumcised, barbaric, uncivilized, slave, or free. Christ is all that matters, and he lives in all of us. (Colossians 3:5-11)

I am not going to lie; before, when I read a verse, I would look at it and think, *Oh my gosh, how can I do this?* and I would already feel defeated. But the New Testament told me! I put my faith in Jesus, I abide in Jesus, and I become aware of Jesus! Like Colossians says, when my faith grows *in* Him, I begin to overflow with thankfulness *to* Him. I love the picture it paints of letting our roots grow down in Him.

You can see that this is such a process! Think about the process of flowers being planted and then blooming. We may plant seeds, but we do not force or control the growth; that is not our part. So, similar to Christ, we sow by our walk with Him. As we trust, He shows up; and as He shows up, we get thankful. We get thankful as we praise, and our roots grow deeper. Our love grows stronger, we are less shakable, and our identity is rooted in Christ.

Instead of making the mistake and then getting right back up, I kind of wallowed. It was hard to shut the voice of the Enemy out long enough to hear the Holy Spirit's guiding and encouraging voice telling me to get back up again. This can put you into a destructive cycle. When you listen to the Enemy, it is not encouraging; it is discouraging.

This cycle must be broken! You do not want to fall into the trap of thinking, *What's the point? I already messed up, so let me do more damage.* Remember, a righteous man may fall seven times, but he always gets back up!

> For though the righteous fall seven times,
> they rise again. (Proverbs 24:16a NIV)

Don't let the Enemy keep you down. Turn to God. I heard someone say once that sometimes your one hundred percent on some days is sixty percent, and that is okay. Don't give up and don't give in. Tell the devil to shut up, and keep doing the next right thing. Keep in mind that sometimes things are a process. Sometimes you do not get the results you want right away—even in yourself. It is a good thing to look back and be able to see that you are improving. I am not going backward. As long as I am moving forward in something, I can give myself grace to say that it is okay. I am proud of how far I have come on this journey to freedom, and God has the same for you!

Chapter 5: A New Hope

Hope and fear. That is a weird combination, I know. At the beginning of this book, I mentioned the very real thoughts of wondering about my salvation and if God accepts me. I was beginning to get gloomy thoughts about Jesus's return because I was afraid I would not get to go! I have felt this in moments when I made mistakes and was going through difficulty. I have had these thoughts when I did not measure up to my—or even God's—expectations. I have had these thoughts turn to fear when I moved forward into new levels.

I need to allow myself to have an eager hope and expectation of the Lord and His return!

I am so thankful for other believers encouraging and reminding me that a person with Jesus does not think that way. I have Jesus. The fact that I am afraid to be without Him is the fear of the Lord. I need to allow myself to have an eager hope and expectation of the Lord and His return! It anchors me!

> This hope is a strong and trustworthy anchor for our souls. It leads us through the curtain into God's inner sanctuary. (Hebrews 6:19)

Instead of letting this hope anchor my soul, I felt like a ship at sea, not knowing where safety was and not knowing if I would be tipped and become a ship at the bottom of the ocean. While I think it is good to self-reflect, I believe it can also turn into an irrational fear that the Enemy likes to use to trap the children of God.

> For God in all his fullness was pleased to live in Christ, and through him God reconciled everything to himself. He made peace with everything in heaven and on earth by means of Christ's blood on the cross. This includes you who were once far away from God. You were his enemies, separated from him by your evil thoughts and actions. Yet now he has reconciled you to himself through the death of Christ in his physical body. As a result, he has brought you into his own presence, and you are holy and blameless as you stand

before him without a single fault. But you must continue to believe this truth and stand firmly in it. Don't drift away from the assurance you received when you heard the Good News. The Good News has been preached all over the world, and I, Paul, have been appointed as God's servant to proclaim it. (Colossians 1:19-23)

God disciplines those He loves. I think that since coming to Christ, after the first month or so, I began to see what I needed to work on, which was a lot! I mean, twenty-one years of living for myself, the world, and the devil. When I began to walk with the Lord, I grew so much, and I was very thankful that I was really living! It was like seeing color for what felt like the first time. I was enjoying the freedom of the Lord, but the Enemy crept in again. I began to get overwhelmed, and I took that yolk of slavery and put it back on myself. I saw my failures and mistakes as signs that I could not be God's child, and hopelessness set in.

I feel deeply about this. I was so afraid of falling away that I began to push myself away. But God! It wasn't until recently, when I was taking communion with my mom, that God brought some profound things to my mind. I began to journal, and I heard the Lord say, "This shows that I love you." He reveals this because He wants to heal us. I stole that from my pastor who I am sure stole it from another pastor! It's okay because it is true, and it brings us full circle from the beginning of this book.

Sanctification is different from salvation. Think about it; when we are born again, we become a child of God. Children need to be taught because they do not know everything. I think about when I took math in school. I would do well, especially in class and with teacher assistance, but then I would fail a test. They did not kick me out of the school for that. I was a student, and I got taught more! It was a bit uncomfortable, embarrassing, and tedious to have to redo the work, but it would not cause me to lose my status as a student.

It is the same in our walk with God: He teaches us, we test, we pass or fail, and depending upon our result, we move forward or go around the same mountain. Hopefully, we get uncomfortable enough to learn and not allow the pressure to make us quit. As long as we do not quit and turn our back on God, we are still His children.

Again, it comes back to a good Father. A good Father reveals, but He also leads, teaches, corrects, and walks with you. I am not alone, and my Father knows what is best for me. I want to let Him lead me. I have not always been the best daughter—I still am not. My first instinct can be to run or hide. I was a chronic runaway from age fourteen to age seventeen, but now I choose to stay. Now I know that my heavenly Father wants to love me to life! I am no longer afraid, because His perfect love casts out all fear (1 John 4:18 NKJV).

Chapter 5: A New Hope

We read in Romans:

> For all who are led by the Spirit of God
> are children of God. So you have not re-
> ceived a spirit that makes you fearful
> slaves. Instead, you received God's Spirit
> when he adopted you as his own children.
> Now we call him, "Abba, Father." For his
> Spirit joins with our spirit to affirm that we
> are God's children. And since we are his
> children, we are his heirs. In fact, togeth-
> er with Christ we are heirs of God's glory.
> But if we are to share his glory, we must
> also share his suffering. (Romans 8:14-17)

I want to touch on the topic of abiding. This is not
an excuse to go on doing what we are doing; it is a call
to allow Him to change our heart, which makes obeying
Him something we now do out of love and relationship
rather than feeling like we are fighting tooth and nail to
obey. Jesus tells us all about this process:

> I am the true vine, and my Father is the
> gardener. He cuts off every branch in me
> that bears no fruit, while every branch that
> does bear fruit he prunes so that it will be
> even more fruitful. You are already clean
> because of the word I have spoken to you.
> Remain in me, as I also remain in you.
> No branch can bear fruit by itself; it must

remain in the vine. Neither can you bear fruit unless you remain in me.

I am the vine; you are the branches. If you remain in me and I in you, you will bear much fruit; apart from me you can do nothing. If you do not remain in me, you are like a branch that is thrown away and withers; such branches are picked up, thrown into the fire and burned. If you remain in me and my words remain in you, ask whatever you wish, and it will be done for you. This is to my Father's glory, that you bear much fruit, showing yourselves to be my disciples.

As the Father has loved me, so have I loved you. Now remain in my love. If you keep my commands, you will remain in my love, just as I have kept my Father's commands and remain in his love. I have told you this so that my joy may be in you and that your joy may be complete. My command is this: Love each other as I have loved you. (John 15:1-12 NIV)

I love this passage because it is so rich. Jesus begins by telling us that if we remain in Him, He remains in us. Some versions have the word *abide.* Something happens when we spend time with Jesus; He begins in us a process called pruning, which sounds like sanctification.

In John 13:10, Jesus lets us know that we have already had that initial cleansing, while John 15 talks of the continual cleansing. According to the Blue Letter Bible (referring to Him taking away branches that do not bear fruit),

> Takes away is more accurately translated as lifts up…Those caring for ancient grape vines made sure to lift them up off the ground so that they might get more sun and bear fruit better.[2]

This is what Jesus is doing in our lives, and this is our hope. He is lifting us up, calling us higher, and empowering us to be obedient to Him. This can only come from a connection with Him.

> "For I know the plans I have for you," says the LORD. "They are plans for good and not for disaster, to give you a future and a hope." (Jeremiah 29:11)

---

2. Guzik, D. "The Departing Jesus teaches His Disciples About Life In Him." (Blue Letter Bible) August, 2022. https://www.blueletter-bible.org/comm/guzik_david/study-guide/john/john-15.cfm

Chapter 6: A New Purpose

This chapter is short but impactful. In the beginning of this book, and up until this chapter, my story was one of not personally knowing Christ; and because of that, not knowing my identity I had with Him. From my perspective, my mistakes became me, my lifestyle became me, and I had nothing to cling to—my identity was not a child of God. The acts of sin led me into a lifestyle of sin, only pulling me further away from God's love, forgiveness, and healing power. The thing I needed most was Jesus, but I ran from Him. I did not know that my sins were a reflection of an unhealed self.

My theology was that I did bad, so I am bad, and I cannot be on Team Jesus. But that is very far from the truth. Jesus wants to meet us in our mess. He is the God that turns things around for us. He is in the business of healing broken people. This next section is a display of how in my own mistakes, as a child of God, fully knowing who I am, God was able to keep me. Something that would have sent me off the deep end in the past was able to be turned into a part of my story. I was able to receive God's mercy through repentance, and I fell in love with Him all over again.

His mercy and grace are not for perfect people. They are for the broken who need him. After all, this book is not for the perfect; this is for the people who are imperfect but have a heart after God. It is not a license to sin. It is for everyone who will take His grace and receive it to move in a new direction—repentance.

Don't overcomplicate it. Turn from your sin, and turn to Jesus! Let Him heal you, and let go of doubt so you can trust. And if you are not there yet, just know that God is waiting for you to say yes to Him. He is a patient God. You are still here because He is not done with you! He will not turn his back on someone who is turning to Him. The thing I am absolutely not saying is to go in with this mindset: *I can sin all I want and then just ask for forgiveness*. What I am saying is similar to what we read in 1 John:

> My little children (believers, dear ones), I am writing you these things so that you will not sin *and* violate God's law. And if anyone sins, we have an Advocate [who will intercede for us] with the Father: Jesus Christ the righteous [the upright, the just One, who conforms to the Father's will in every way—purpose, thought, and action]. (1 John 2:1 AMP)

I am not going to say that my sin did not have consequences, because it did. I had to go through more healing. I could not keep doing the same things I was doing; I had to deal with shame and the impact my sin had on my relationships. So what did I do to put myself in this position?

I had sex outside of marriage—as a born-again, set-free, delivered Christian. I willfully did it. I was in rebellion. I knew this was not me; I was acting out of character because that was not who I was anymore. It took a little bit to step out and let go of what felt good to my flesh, and that was hard. It was not easy to let go, but by God's grace, I was able to have a moment of clarity and make a clean break with what I was doing.

God brought me through all of these trials and gave me a purpose, and He desperately wants to do the same for you!

Once I stopped running and confessed and repented, I did not doubt that I was still His daughter. I had done the thing that I did not think I was even capable of as a saved woman of God. I had just done what was the worst sin in my eyes, yet I had a sense that He still loved me, cared about me, and was waiting for my return. Tell me that is not a good Father! If you read the rest of my story, you know that was not my method of operation. My m.o. was to doubt that I was a child of God for breathing wrong. In the past, this sort of situation would have taken me out for the count. Not knowing my identity in Christ is what led to a meth addiction at seventeen years old. God brought me through all of these trials and gave me a purpose, and He desperately wants to do the same for you! Then He will use you to help others.

> But you are not like that, for you are a chosen people. You are a royal priesthood, a holy nation, God's very own possession. As a result, you can show others the goodness of God, for he called you out of the darkness into his wonderful light. (1 Peter 2:9)

Chapter 7: A New Future

I would like to end this book by coming full circle. Knowing what I know now, it is only because of the Holy Spirit—His mercy and grace—and the body of Christ that I am still here. This should have taken me out, but God kept me, and I had some groundwork of my identity in Christ. The ability to evaluate my sin, as a daughter if Christ, changed everything for me. I was able to process why it happened. It really came down to a lack of trusting what God had said. Once I stopped trusting His guidance, I leaned on my own understanding.

> Trust in the LORD with all your heart; do not depend on your own understanding. (Proverbs 3:5)

I acted according to my flesh, let go of my boundaries, and I fell into weakness.

During this brief period, I told a friend about it. As I told her the reality that I was choosing to ignore God's direction, she never forced me to turn around; she just said, "God is ready when you are." One thing though is that I stayed pretty honest with myself—I knew that I was in rebellion. I had a couple of moments of denial, but overall, I knew. At that point, I was sure that I had lost everything—my character, trust, friends, accountability, my church—so I ignored my duties and accountability. That only lasted a week until they caught on to me. I was not met with the hammer, though, like I expected. I was met with a grace I did not even know existed.

Throughout my whole Christian walk, the biggest display of mercy in my life was when I transformed from a sinner to a saint. While I was a sinner, Christ died for me.

> But God showed His great love for us
> by sending Christ to die for us while we
> were still sinners. (Romans 5:8)

I had not yet experienced it in my actual walk as a saint. When I let accountability in, I was not met with, "Oh, poor thing, you didn't know better." It was, "How did this happen? How can we restore you? We still love you, so don't let the Enemy lie to you to bring you deeper into his pit." I thank God that my leaders loved me but did not sugarcoat the reality of my actions, and never once did they tell me that I could go on sinning. They never condemned me; they helped restore me by telling me the truth about how my sin could have easily taken me out and others also. I was told I was being selfish. Willful and blatant sin cannot be forgiven if you do not want it to be; and you don't if you are unrepentant. I thought, *What?! Just like that? You don't know what I have done.*

Jesus forgave me, restored me, and put my feet in a new direction.

It took the courage of confession for a moment of clarity to come in so I could realize what I was doing. This life that God has given me is not worth throwing away like I had at seventeen. Yes, measures were put into place to allow me to heal; they were not to punish me but to restore me. What kind of love is that? All I can do is be grateful. I could not help wanting to turn my life around. I could not help wanting to do better. It was Jesus! His grace and mercy were displayed through my church at a time when I felt I did not deserve them. They were so freely given that day, if I would only receive them. I did not have to do much. I confessed, repented, and received. Jesus forgave me, restored me, and put my feet in a new direction.

Can I tell you that if you are a child of God who loves Him, He will use everything for your good—I mean EVERYTHING! Even our biggest mistakes. This situation—although painful, not only for myself but those I hurt in the process of choosing my own way—God allowed me to restore. He was still with me to help me get back on track. Man, am I grateful for the Holy Spirit!

I came out of that with more gratitude, more compassion, more trust, and a reboot in understanding His grace and mercy for His children. And I came out of it with a mission to share this good news with as many people as possible. In my final words, I want to tell you this: Before you ever accept that you will live in sin forever or that you are too far gone, get to know Jesus, and He will change you. I pray He opens your eyes so you will not lean on your own understanding but run to Him—even if you feel like you can't.

If you already know Christ, evaluate this as a child of God. How would a good Father approach you? With love and grace, but He is not okay with letting you settle for less than His best for your life—though it is YOUR choice. If you are not ready to repent, just know that He is waiting. And while, yes, He is waiting, you are not promised tomorrow. It could be your last day today, so do not wait too long.

Take advantage of moments of clarity because we have no guarantee they will always be there. The devil is out to steal, kill, and destroy. Sin does separate us from God, and eventually, it will be harder to hear Him tell you to come home. Don't let your heart become hardened.

We must desire God's ways above our own

We have to come to a place of desperation where we say, "God, I don't want this. I know it doesn't align with what You say, so help me desire Your way because You know best." My favorite verse is from the book of Jeremiah:

> "In those days when you pray, I will listen. If you look for me wholeheartedly, you will find me. I will be found by you," says the LORD. "I will end your captivity and restore your fortunes." (Jeremiah 29:12-14)

This is my favorite verse because it was that one prayer I prayed that changed the trajectory of my life. I believe it was then that I first saw sin for what it is, and my God stepped in. I had finally gotten to the point that I was sick of my sin, and I understood the reality of what needing a Savior really means. I was at the end of myself. Today, He is my Lord, which means I follow His voice and plan, surrendering my life to Him to the best of my ability.

The great thing is that I don't have to allow my life to get to the place it was before I first gave my heart to Him. I do this by living in daily surrender—and you can do it too. Never doubt that you have to do this alone because Jesus wants to do it with you. With man it is impossible, but with God all things are possible (Matthew 19:26).

You can live the life that He has called you to live—only believe!

If you don't know Jesus Christ, I want to invite you to pray a prayer that will help you begin your journey with Him.

Hi, Jesus, I need You. I recognize that I am a sinner who needs a Savior. I need You not only now but for the rest of my days. Help me to let go of the ideas, actions, and sin that have led me away from You. Change me from the inside out. I humble myself right now and say that Your ways are higher than mine. Please begin to change the desires of my heart and lead me on the narrow path. Jesus, I believe that You are the only way to God the Father and to heaven, and that Your death on the cross was the full payment for my sin. Lord, thank You for washing me clean and wiping away my sin and shame. I turn from evil and turn to You. Help me to put my faith and trust in You daily, knowing that today is the first day of my new life. In Your name I pray. Amen.

About the Author

Raven Kask is a woman who has experienced the transformative power of God, and she has a burden to help others find new life and freedom through Jesus Christ. Like many today, she struggled with insecurity and a lack of identity—while growing up in church. This caused her to search for fulfillment in other ways until she reached the end of herself. With nowhere else to turn, she cried out to God; in His mercy, He healed her heart and changed her life. Her message is that we can all experience a blessed and victorious life knowing we belong *to* and *with* Christ. Raven and her family live in the Pacific Northwest. Raven can be contacted at childofgodraven@gmail.com.